Chinese Water Dragons as Pets

Caring For Your Chinese Water Dragons

Chinese Water Dragons General Info, Purchasing, Care, Cost, Keeping, Health, Supplies, Food, Breeding and More Included!

By Lolly Brown

Foreword

Upon setting sights on the little green Chinese Water Dragons, countless reptile aficionados' hearts were captured and had since made the popularity of these tiny bright reptiles heighten. It is one of the many lizard species hobbyists and enthusiasts fall in love with and choose to take in and raise it in captivity.

These generally docile, moderately even-tempered, very active, and rambunctiously playful Chinese Water Dragons are natives of the balmy, tropical regions of Thailand, Cambodia, Vietnam and Southeastern China.

The Chinese water dragon will need the mature commitment of a keeper in terms of its care and wellness. For you, the budding reptile keeper guardian, we have compiled a world of useful information on the history, the care for, the husbandry, the requirements, the habitat, the nourishment of, and everything in between!

Table of Contents

Introduction

Imagine the duo of an utterly handsome male and an equally gorgeous female Chinese Water Dragon basking on a fully decked out vivarium set low on the floor for better viewing. Now open your eyes and stop daydreaming. You've been holding out on yourself too long. Time to get a move on and seek out your very own buddies to take home!

These generally docile, moderately even-tempered, very active, and rambunctiously playful Chinese Water Dragons are natives of the balmy, tropical regions of Thailand, Cambodia, Vietnam and Southeastern China. They have healthy appetites and juicy mealworms, woodworms and insects.

Upon setting sights on the little green Chinese Water Dragons, countless reptile aficionados' hearts were captured and had since made the popularity of these tiny bright reptiles heighten. It is one of the many lizard species hobbyists and enthusiasts fall in love with and choose to take in and raise it in captivity.

For you, the budding reptile keeper guardian, we have compiled a world of useful information on the history, the care for, the husbandry, the requirements, the habitat, the nourishment of, and everything in between you would need to know to get to know and confidently raise a healthy Chinese water dragon or two.

They are also pretty adept with their swimming skills and have been spotted in the wild, and in captivity, to enjoy an occasional refreshing dip, as it swiftly maneuvers its body through the water with its flattened tail swishing on the water surface. When in the face of danger Chinese water dragons take to water in an effort to flee a situation it deems unsafe. This athletic jungle dweller has the ability to stay underwater for extended periods lasting up to 25 minutes!

As much as they enjoy a cool moist body, Chinese Water Dragons have also been spotted digging burrows and living in the sandy regions of their native Southeast Asian countries. These bright green water dragons are arboreal reptiles with an innate need to climb, scamper and scurry on and off tree branches with the use of its fast legs, long tail and a "third eye" located between its eyes. This special eye, which looks more like a marking, is believed to help it sense predatory presence thereby avoiding danger and being a large animal's dinner. This third eye of theirs is also said to help the Chinese water dragon in thermo-regulating its body temperature - a very special, very unique and highly functional feature indeed!

Temperaments of wild and captive Chinese water dragons are understandably unlike each other due to the differences of environment and exposure. Aside from fleeing up and away on trees, and separating itself from predators with a small body of water, our green buddy here uses its tail and whips it about as a form of defense.

You, our budding reptile keeper, will get to know more details about them as you read further.

Chapter One: Biological Information

This chapter begins your in depth research on the Chinese Water Dragon as you start your quest on learning all about your desired reptile pet. To help you get ready for what promises to be an unforgettable milestone meeting, allow us to shed light on comprehensive facts about the Chinese water dragon and everything you would need to know about this usually jolly, green reptile, in preparation for a fitting homecoming welcome. This proactive step of learning is a smart way to start a promisingly fruitful friendship.

Getting to know the originations of your pet and how it lives in its natural habitat gives you, as its future keeper, an advantage of understanding the biological makeup of the Chinese water dragon allowing you to recognize and identify details that may be missed by an uninformed would-be keeper.

What are Chinese Water Dragons?

Meet this bright green fella of the reptile kingdom, which has captured many hobbyists and reptile enthusiasts' hearts - The Chinese Water Dragon, also scientifically known as *Physignathus cocincinus*.

Water dragons are arboreal tree huggers who enjoy spending a good part of their time flanked with trees, bushes and greenery. This bit of dragon fact makes them skilled climbers, leapers and jumpers. Dragons thrive best and typically prefer hanging around areas where the average level of humidity ranges around 80 percent during mornings and around 60 percent during evening with temperatures averaging somewhere between 75 to 85 degrees Fahrenheit.

Their common name gives clue that water dragons like spending an equally good chunk of their lives in water hence they gravitate where small bodies of water are permanent and constant. Dragons may have found the perfect nirvana amidst rainforests, swampy marsh lands, beside ponds, by lake sides, and on river banks where home and territory is established.

Did I mention that they are pretty fine swimmers too? Well, they are. As fast and as graceful as these daredevils use their well-developed feet to scamper off branches and leap into water below indicate of its equally magnificent swimming abilities. Water dragons possess a seemingly endless list of talents, abilities and features, which we shall enumerate and describe in detail as we go along.

Origin and Distribution

The water dragon and its kin can be found near the water channels of Cambodia, Laos, Vietnam, Thailand and Southern China. These brightly hued reptiles prefer to stay close to streams and lakes in the rainforests of Southeast Asia.

Size and Physical Appearance

Reportedly an extremely pleasant reptile to care for by some, said to be feisty and tempestuous by others, expect keeper experiences living with their water dragon to be worlds apart. If you think about it, just like humans, they too are unique individuals. One thing that most keepers probably agree with is that Chinese water dragons are undoubtedly an attractive water dragon specimen sporting its full green body armor with interesting shocks of bright colors which starkly contrast its green physique.

As teeny hatchlings, they come scampering out into the world at an impressive length of 5 to 6 inches from snout to tail tip! On the top surface of its body is painted by nature with a brownish green color. Its abdominal parts are a pale green that recedes to chalk white. On the sides of the length of its body run light stripes of either beige or white, giving it an appearance of a classic American car with streaks of lightning. It's long tail, which it uses to defend itself or at the very least swish sharply to show displeasure, is banded with colors of green and brown. A short snout with huge, large eyes on the sides of its head completes the impressive appearance of the Chinese Water Dragon.

As the water dragon grows it will shed its skin a few times. When it comes to about 10 inches in length a magnificent transformation happens to it. The upper body of the water dragon color morphs into a bright, brilliant green color subtly ranging from a soft mint green, a calm turquoise to a bold aqua. You will learn that the color play doesn't end there, if you read on.

Both juvenile and adult Chinese water dragons have hued throats of colors that starkly contrast its predominantly green body. The color of its neck is delivered by nature, on a timely schedule, in a hue-range of faint yellow, an orange sunset, a sunrise peach, bright pink, hot fuchsia to a rich, deep purple.

The triangular head of the Chinese water dragon gets pretty large as it grows. Big round scales run along the bottom of its mouth and sharply tapers off ending with pointed scales on each side just where its neck and head converge. A dark strip of line hugs the corners of the water dragon's eyes leading up to end at the ears.

It has a wide, thick, tongue which has a sticky surface and a fork tipped end, two features of its tongue that comes in handy when capturing and fastening onto prey. Chinese water dragons have small pointed teeth which they not only use to dine on an omnivorous diet but also to bite with on occasion.

Adult females and males both have properly-developed nuchal crests, which are a fancy way of describing horny thorns, just above their necks with the male's thorns raised higher and notably longer than those of the females. Male Chinese water dragons have quite a unique feature; a mid-sagittal crest, set between its eyes and located directly at the top of its large triangular head; this is one reptile who truly DOES HAVE a third eye! The parietal eye is believed to help water dragons (and other equally unique reptiles) sense light in its varying degrees in order to thermoregulate. The mid sagittal crest helps the water dragon decide on a suitable basking spot, and alternatively, sense waning light giving it cue to seek shelter for the night.

They have strong and muscular legs with their front legs notably more slender compared to the chunky pair that carry their hind. Its front legs are perfect to use like hands when climbing, using them to grab onto branches whilst their powerful back legs kick-hoist their weight up. Their strong back legs are great tools for jumping on and leaping off objects they clamber onto. All four feet of the Chinese water dragon has five toes with all four middle toes longer than the rest.

Growth Rate

The adult male Chinese water dragon grows to a length of about 3 feet with adult females coming in a tad shorter at an average length of 2 feet. Making up the water dragons length is their brown and green banded tail are flattened laterally and trails to a fine-tipped point which makes up the majority of its length.

Its color banded, laterally flat and extremely powerful and utilitarian tail is not only a great rudder for the water dragon when it goes for a swim, and its tail is also used to balance itself as it traverses from tree to tree. The water dragon also uses it as leverage when climbing. A tail of many trades, the water dragon uses it like a whip to thwack at eager would-be predators, attackers and yes, even keepers have not been spared.

Most Chinese water dragons have the similar appearance of a female dragon. It is only when males grow to a length of 14 to 16 that gender becomes apparent when the male dragons develop larger heads, drooped jowls and a nuchal crest set higher. Almost every part of the male Chinese water dragon is larger than the females with the last body part comparison being the larger male femoral pores compared to those of the female water dragon.

Dragons are generally considered mature and ready to breed when it reaches its two year life mark and its body length has reached two feet.

Chinese Water Dragon Lifespan

In the wild the Chinese water dragon has been noted to enjoy a longevity of about or a little over decade. In the wild, water dragons are obviously exposed to a variety of situations. It would have to forage and hunt for its food with the probability of not yielding enough to satiate hunger. Not having enough to eat, not getting the proper balance of nutrients would not immediately result in starvation, but malnourishment is a slow process of deficiency.

Predators are another reason for a water dragon to live a shorter life span. Aside from the competition of other water dragons seeking out the same food, predators are real danger water dragons have to face.

Sickness and disease in the wild is obviously something water dragons will have to endure on their own sans medical attention.

In captivity, the length of life expectancy of the water dragon is radically higher. With medical care from an expert herp vet, the dragons have the chance and luxury of getting the detailed health attention they need,

With keeper guardians attending to their care and the provision of food water dragons are spared from the hard work of having to hunt and forage for food. Given optimal care, water dragons in captivity have been reported to survive anywhere from 11 to 15 years. Those under the care of zoos can live even longer with one reportedly at 17 years!

Chapter Two: Chinese Water Dragons as Pets

Ever since the first hobbyist realized the joys of taking in reptiles and amphibians as pets, the reptile hobby has been a-buzz with requests and sometimes, demands for Chinese water dragons which sadly could be one of the reasons why many Chinese water dragons are still hunted and caught in the wild for the pet trade industry.

The *Physignathus cocincinus,* or more widely known as the Chinese Water Dragon, is also known by other names such as the Green Water Dragon or the Asian Water Dragon.

These tiny little bug-eyes reptiles are natives of the Southeast Asian mainland's like, southern China, Thailand, Cambodia and Vietnam.

Consider this book a start-up guide for you, our budding reptile keeper, to exploit. We encourage you to pour through these pages, dog-ear pages, underline passages and extend your research further beyond the content between these covers.

Every pet chosen by man has its emergence in nature and a beginning of sharing space and life with humans. The advent of some of these chosen pets can be vague and murky at times, however, what is important is your decidedly steadfast commitment to giving your reptile ward the best possible care whilst under your guardianship.

What Makes It a Great Pet

Tales of the Chinese water dragon's temperament are aplenty. Keeper experiences will vary largely perhaps because like us humans they too, as many outward similarities they may share with their sort, are still individuals with unique traits, moods, behaviors, quirks, oddities and temperaments. Improper handling could also be suspect when keepers talk of protestations when it acts out whilst being held, carried or given a routine physical exam.

They are awesome pets to keep because of their even-temperedness, their adaptability and uncomplicated needs. As long as the keeper guardian attends to them and checks that the water dragon has no immediate requirements, they remain happy loungers, baskers, and players.

The Chinese Water Dragon make for excellent reptile pets for individuals who already has some experience caring for a reptile, and excellent ones for the more advanced, more seasoned herpetoculturist, since they are generally friendly, as far as reptiles are concerned. The water dragons of Asia are not finicky but they do require a great deal of time and resources and a potential keeper guardian of one should be ready for the long haul care and responsibilities that come with raising a Chinese water dragon.

Pros and Cons of Owning One

Reptiles, in captivity, had it tough in the past because there were only a handful of veterinarians who specialized in their care. Time has thankfully changed in the past decade or so with more medical vets recognizing the growing need for experts in the field of reptile care there are currently more of these specialized experts in service than before. It is still not as easy to find these medical experts and a keeper guardian will have to do the necessary homework and care to get the services of one, but it is indeed more possible now, more than ever.

The Chinese water dragon will need the mature commitment of a keeper in terms of its care and wellness. The water dragon will require a number of conditions met to be able to thrive optimally under captive care and the future keeper has to have a good head on their shoulders to take claim of the required needs to be a prime keeper of this beautiful species of nature.

Legal Requirements and CITES Law

The Convention on International Trade in Endangered Species of Wild Fauna and Flora is an international agreement amongst world governments that helps ensure that the trade of plants and wild animals internationally is regulated, monitored and documented. All these regulations were put in place to make sure that plant specimens and animal species survival is not threatened with endangerment of extinction.

Initial ideas back in the 1960 were relatively new and vague but as the years progressed the need for stricter laws and bylaws became clearer. With the growing trade of flora and fauna becoming more prevalent and widespread, it was important for a governing body to set stricter laws and trade regulations to make sure that the dangers of animal and plant extinction is curbed.

It is estimated that the annual trade of plants and animals amount to billions of dollars. A very diverse trade of live plants and animals as well as a varied assortment of products derived from wildlife which includes exotic leather goods, wooden musical instruments, timber, tourist curios, food products, and medicines.

The exploitation levels of some animal and plant species were staggering as well as the trade in them, coupled with numerous other factors, like loss of habitat, is capable of dangerously depleting animal and plant populations and has even brought some species dangerously close to extinction. A lot of wildlife species currently in trade are not endangered, but the reality of an agreement to make certain of the sustainability of the trade is vital in order to protect these resources for the future.

The procedure of stating a declaration to be tied into the provisions of CITES is called 'ratification', 'acceptance', 'approval' or 'accession'. Ratification, acceptance and approval are legally equivalent actions. However these are only applicable in connection to the States which signed the Convention when it was available and open for signature, between 3 March 1973 and 31 December 1974. Except for China, all the other countries of the Chinese Water Dragons originations are governed by CITES regulations.

There are plant and animal species and specimens listed on the endangered list which under special circumstances like medical research, which can possibly get approval for trade if given approval provided that grant of authorization of export and import permits are secured. There would still be a number of exceptions and general prohibition to be considered and followed even after the fact of being given a green light.

The Chinese water dragons is not currently listed on any of the CITES lists of specimens with restrictions but it is still important for a keeper to understand both import and export trading laws in their home countries regarding the trade, transport and sale of Chinese water dragons.

Myths about Chinese Water Dragons

Chinese dragons, in ancient lore, are often related to and associated with water and rain as well as lakes and rivers. These dragons are lauded and said to be divine mythical creatures which, when present, brings about ultimate good fortune of abundance and prosperity. Not at like the aspect of negativity associated with Western Dragons, most Eastern Dragons are described to be beautiful, friendly, and wise. They are the said to be the angels of the Orient. These dragons are not shunned with hatred but are instead are loved and worshipped. Shrines and temples have been erected to pay respect and give honor to them, because it is them who control the rain, rivers, lakes, and seas.

In fact, China's four great rivers were named after Dragons. The Heilongjian or the Black Dragon located in the far north of the country, the Huanghe, or Yellow River, which is in central China, the Changjiang, also known as Yangtze or Long River is located farther south and last but not at all the least, is the Zhujiang, or Pearl, which is situated in the very far south of China.

The Lung or the Chinese Dragon is also a symbol of power and excellence, boldness and valiancy, perseverance and heroism, divinity and nobility. A dragon is said to be able to overcome any and all obstacles until success is achieved. A Dragon is optimistic, intelligent, energetic, decisive, and ambitious.

These dragons are mostly associated with the emperors and royalty and they are closely associated with the image of a dragon. Before history commenced, China's first emperor, Fu Hsi was said to possess a dragon's' tail and his successor, Shen Nung, was told to have been sired by a dragon. The Lung or the Imperial Dragon possesses five claws and not the usual four. The ordinary dragon or mang has temporal power with no spiritual prowess. The Lung or Dragon King gave orders for the Emperor by moving in four directions simultaneously. The fifth direction, which is in connection with the fifth claw, is the center where he stays and remains.

The Dragon brings upon and breathes out the essence of life, in the form of its celestial breath, known to and described by many as sheng chi. The Dragon yields life and gifts its power in the form of the seasons of the year, bringing forth water from rain, warmth emitted from the sunshine of the sun, wind from the vast seas and soil from the ground of the earth. The Dragon is the ultimate depiction of the forces of Mother Nature, the greatest divine force on Earth.

The Chinese Dragon is frequently displayed and portrayed as the symbol of divine protection and vigilance. The Chinese Dragon is thought to be the most Supreme Being amongst all creatures of the Earth. The Chinese Dragon has the ability to reside in the seas, soar up to the heavens and coiled up in the land in the shape of mountains. Being the divine mythical creature, the Chinese Dragon has the power to ward off wandering evil spirits, give protection to the innocent and grant safety to all who hold the Dragon's emblem. The Chinese Dragon is perceived and looked upon as the ultimate symbol of Good Fortune.

Chinese Water Dragons vs. Australian Water Dragons

Here's a bit of information about two types of water dragons that would be great information for new reptile keepers to understand.

The Australian Water Dragon, or the *Intellagama lesueurii,* was once scientifically known as the *Physignathus lesueurii*; categorized as an Australian water dragon subspecies include the eastern water dragon and Gippsland water dragon. These water dragons from Australia are arboreal agamid reptiles which originate from Australia from the region of Victoria all the way northward to

Queensland with a possibility of a small population introduced on the south-east South Australian coast.

These water dragons from Australia possess powerful, long limbs with very strong claws the water dragon's use for climbing. It has a tail which is laterally-compressed which aids for swimming. These water dragons have very prominent nuchal and vertebral crests. The nuchal crest is a row of horn-like thorns or spikes located at the center of its back which starts at its head and runs all the way down its spine and notably gets smaller as it reaches the base of the water dragon's tail.

The total average length of Australian water dragons, including its tail is about 2 feet for females with adult males a tad longer at about 3 feet with an average weight of roughly around 1 kilo. Males display bolder hues and like their Asian counterparts, Australian water dragons too have larger heads than the female dragons. Juvenile Australian Water Dragon's colors are less distinct and come into full spectrum when maturity is reached.

The water dragon from Australia is also the only species of the genus Intellagama. Two of the subspecies of Intellagama are the Eastern water dragon. The Eastern water dragon displays neck colors tending towards white, yellow and red with a dark band around its eyes.

In contrast, the Gippsland Water Dragon does not possess these eye markings; possessing dark bands on either side of its throat instead which are blotched with orange, yellow or blue.

These two subspecies sport similar overall colors of light greenish grey with black bands that run across their backs, legs and tails. These water dragons have a special ability of gradually changing skin coloration as a way of camouflage. During periods of growth, these Australian water dragon subspecies will shed their skin.

Extremely elusive and shy in the wild, Australian water dragons are much more receptive to human presence and handling when in captivity and show behavior of ready adaptation to social settings in gardens and parks frequented by humans.

These water dragons are swift runners and deft climbers specially when in the face of danger and potential predators, seeking cover in dense vegetation or leap-dropping from a tree branch into water. These dragons are able to swim under water, unlike their Asian counterparts who skim the surface of water - and settle on the floor of shallow lakes and creeks for up to an impressive 90 minutes, avoiding detection.

Male and female Australian water dragons have typical agamid traits like basking, head-bobbing and arm-waving. Swift arm-waving is a sign of dominance, with slow arm-waving signaling submission. Male water dragons from these Australian regions are highly territorial and where there is a higher population of their sort, males usually display aggression against other males by fighting, chasing and posturing.

The water dragons of Australia which live in cooler regions hibernate over winter. During spring season, usually sometime in early October, the female Australian water dragon would excavate a burrow of 10 to 15 centimeters in depth and would lie anywhere from 8 to 18 eggs. Her nest is typically in an area where sun exposure is rich and on soft or sandy soil.

Once the female lays her eggs she precedes to backfill the burrowed chamber with soil and covers the area with loose debris she collects for this purpose of extra protection. Temperature dependent, hatchling gender is determined by the temperature of the nest site. Once hatched, the young Australian water dragons hang around the burrow entrance for a short period of time before breaking free of the chamber and leave the nest. Once out, the lot prefer to group together away from the mature water dragon population.

Living up to its name, Australian water dragons are associated with water and are semi-aquatic by nature. They are spotted where water can be found like, rivers, lakes, creeks and other bodies of water where basking spots are aplenty, usually with branches overhanging the water, where there are rocks and in an sun exposed or filtered area. The sort is typical in the sections of rainforest in the Brisbane Botanic Gardens, Mount Cootha in Queensland, where a monument for them was built.

Anecdotal reports say that a small colony of Australian water dragons live on the Sixth Creek in the Forest Range area of South Australia. This small colony is supposed to have been introduced to that region, which is hundreds of miles outside of their natural range, by a reptile enthusiast back in the 1980's.

The water dragons from Australia are prey to snakes, cats, dogs, foxes and birds. The younger nestlings and smaller juvenile water dragons are vulnerable to predators like currawongs, butcherbirds and kookaburras as well as other carnivorous birds. They are equally prone to road kill accidents because the attraction of warm concrete and bitumen for basking purposes.

The diet of the Australian water dragon depends largely on their size. Juveniles and year-old dragons like of feed on small insects like spiders, ants, caterpillars, and crickets. As they grow and get bigger their prey does too. The diet of an adult Australian water dragon would include small rodents like mice with insects still the main choice diet and the most consumed.

Chapter Three: Purchasing and Selecting a Healthy Breed

There are a number of avenues a potential Chinese Water Dragon keepers check out in their pursuit of search of the dragon pet they desire. However, it is also important for the keeper to understand the implications of dealing with any of the places where the Chinese Water Dragons are said to be available.

The next sections in this chapter aims to help the potential sort out the business of where to ask, who to deal with, what the keeper may expect, vital questions the keeper needs to ask, and have answers for and about, regarding the Chinese Water Dragons history.

The potential keeper will also be given an extensive overview of how to spot a healthy - and essentially, a sick - Chinese Water Dragon. This is by no means the end all and be all of your research on its health. We give you strong recommendation to set an appointment with an expert herp veterinarian at this quite early stage so you are aware of what to expect and what is expected of you to give care to a water dragon. The earlier you know what is required of you, the better you will be able to weigh your options, determine your commitment and make a sound decision about acquiring a water dragon.

Where to Buy a Chinese Water Dragons

As mentioned earlier, a potential water dragon keeper guardian has a number of options to explore as they seek out a water dragon to bring home. The following information is not only research we have done for your convenience and information, this section also has been compiled from seasoned Chinese water dragon keepers, herp enthusiasts and reptile afficionado's stories and reports. Aside from seeking the expert advice of an expert herp vet, we also highly encourage you to network with herp experts, reptile keepers and reputable breeders in your locality.

Let's begin with the place most obvious and abounding with information of breeders and locations where Chinese water dragons, the Internet. The World Wide Web is a huge marketplace and you will find a great deal of sites which claim having water dragons under their care.

The concerns about purchasing a Chinese water dragon (or two) online is long. First off, we discourage a potential keeper from buying a reptile pet they have no possibility of physically seeing before closing a deal. We dissuade an online simply because you, as future guardian, will want to be able to see for yourself the physical appearance and condition of the water dragon in question.

Buying online could go smoother at the onset because promises from a stranger are easy to make from a distance. You also want to witness how the water dragon acts, reacts and interacts. Let us say and assume that the person you are dealing with seems to be on the up and up and you are indeed comfortable with all their answers to your questions about the history of the Chinese water dragon under their care, what you will need to consider now is transporting the water dragon from the location of the dealer to your doorstep.

Cost of transporting the animal, for one, is a detail you will have to work out with the online dealer (if you choose this route of purchase), length of time it will take for the water dragon to get to you, and of course the most important is what assurances are given to the safety of the water dragon during transport. These will be another set of procedural steps you will need to monitor and follow, not to mention the additional costs of logistics, along with cargo and handling fees.

Another option you have, but one we discourage, is visiting a pet store. Pet stores usually are usual grounds where illegally shipped in animals are "dumped". The problem with pet stores is that, even with those with the best intentions, pet stores are hardly informed of the history of the animal, location of where they came from, the means of their arrival into the country if native of another, medical history or lack thereof of the animal. These animals are usually placed in an enclosure and housed together in cramped spaces with no regard for compatibility or safety of the animals, which can result in aggressive behavior in the animal.

The options we recommend would be to first get in touch with your local herp organization, or one which is near your location, and make inquiries about reputable Chinese water dragon breeders the organization can recommend to you. Another option is reaching out to seasoned reptile enthusiasts in your locality (which you can research online) and ask for their recommendations and advice of reputable dealers they trust to be upstanding individuals who employ proper and humane breeding methods to produce healthy water dragons.

You may also check out reptile shelters that may have a Chinese Water Dragon in their care. If you decide this to be your choice of avenue to acquiring your water dragon, you will still need to ask pertinent questions about the history of the water dragon like how the dragon came under their possession, reasons why the dragon was handed over to the shelter (was it from an ex-keeper who realized they bit off more than they could chew? Was it because the water dragon displayed more than usual aggression towards people? Did the previous keepers move away and could not bring their pet? Was it because the water dragon was sick? Was the shelter provided documentation of medical procedures the water dragon may have undergone?), and how the water dragon has fared under their care, the diet it is given at the shelter and how it is housed there. You will probably get some of those questions answered, or you won't. Either way, it will be your choice in the end. However you should be realistic about expectations. A previously owned water dragon would have been exposed to a measure of socialization, which is a positive thing. An older, more mature water dragon would be more set in its ways than a young water dragon.

The best option is dealing with a reputed Chinese water dragon breeder in your location or logistically accessible to you. The good news here for you is that, many Chinese water dragon keepers, through years of experience, have been able to fine tune the breeding process of multiplying their collection and would be more than happy to share the joys of raising a Chinese water dragon or two with you.

You should go ahead and ask all pertinent questions like their methods of breeding, what the water dragons are fed, where they are housed, the temperament of the water dragon, its moods, quirks, personality and of course, importantly, the physical condition of the water dragon and its overall wellness. Advantages of dealing with a well-known, reputable and upstanding water dragon breeder are geared toward your favor more as well. Dealing with an upstanding breeder means they have first-hand information about the animal, can answer your questions with ready confidence and transparency and they are able to give assurances and guarantees the places previously mentioned wouldn't.

Another plus about dealing with known water dragon breeders is these breeders will be able to point you in the direction of other water dragon keepers in your area, or those living in nearby areas, with whom you can network and consult with during the early learning stages of being a reptile keeper. Reputed breeders would almost definitely be able to direct you to an expert herp vet who will be a vital consultant and medical provider for your new reptile pet and a valued supporter of your new hobby and role of raising a reptile successfully.

Characteristics of a Healthy Breed

You want to be at the best advantage when you start checking out Chinese water dragons to choose from when you are ready and confident that you have covered all if not most of the important bases in relation to you purchasing, or adopting, a Chinese water dragon. Here are some things you need to know to be able to spot a healthy Chinese water dragon.

- The water dragon is alert and aware of its surroundings and any changes around it

- The water dragon displays a measure of elusiveness but is gradually able to respond to the presence of humans in its presence

- The Chinese water dragon is a healthy eater

- The water dragon takes to water naturally

- Check that there are no areas of discoloration on the body of the water dragon

- Make sure that the water dragon is mobile and is able to move about without difficulty or hindrance

- Check that all of its digits are intact with no injuries

- The eyes of a healthy water dragon is clear, alert and responsive to movement

- Its ears are discharge free

- So are its nostrils free of any discharge

- Scales are not flaking nor does it fall off when handled

- Tail is strong, laterally placed and moves with natural ease

- There should be no signs of nicks, scars, gashes, sores or wounds

- The mouth of the water dragon has no signs of mouth rot

- There are no signs of bacterial fungus or skin infections on the body of the water dragon

- It is not hostile or combative, more than normal

- The Stoll of the water dragon is not loose or watery

Characteristics of a Reputable Breeder

Be informed and make sound decisions about breeders you will potentially be talking to during your search for a water dragon. Here are some important things to remember and consider when talking to breeders.

- Breeders of good reputation will not hesitate to answer any and all questions about the water dragon in question.

- These breeders would have the proper housing equipment for their temporary, transient reptile wards.

- The good breeder would have an expert herp vet on their speed dial

- An upstanding breeder will also have their own set of questions to ask a potential keeper about the home conditions of the buyer.

- They would be more than happy impart important advice and tips to the future keeper not only for their assurance that the reptile is going to be paired with a suitable keeper, but also to ensure the safety and healthy future of the water dragon.

- Breeders of high standards will have a complete and comprehensive record of the water dragons medical history and any procedures and tests it may have already undergone.

- A responsible breeder would also have initiated the initial inoculations needed by the reptile before handing the water dragon over to you.

- A thoughtful breeder would be concerned about the housing requirements of the water dragon and may probe the potential keeper about what measures they have taken to prepare the enclosure of the water dragon

- Breeders with a high recommendation rating would be open to parting with some of supplies you may need to build a better more conducive vivarium to ensure the that comforts of home required by the water dragon is met.

List of Breeders and Rescue Websites

For the convenience of getting you closer to your goal of acquiring a Chinese water dragon, here is a list of online sites which you can start checking individually. Once again, a gentle reminder that we do not advocate or promote purchasing a Chinese water dragon, or any pet for that matter, online without the possibility of being able to see the water dragon for yourself.

Most breeders, you will notice, may also be sellers of supplies you will need to set up your water dragons vivarium. They will also be aware and in close collaboration and contact with reptile pet food suppliers where you can procure your future water dragon's nutritional needs.

This compiled list is aimed to get the gears of looking for your Chinese water dragon in the works. We still strongly suggest that you go beyond this list we have provided and make your own cold calls to get in touch with the people we mentioned earlier in this chapter.

List of Breeders in United States

Snakes at Sunseet
<http://snakesatsunset.com/small-chinese-water-dragon/>

Big Apple Herp
<http://www.bigappleherp.com/Water-Dragon>

Reptile RescueC Org
<http://reptilerescueoc.org/?gclid=CjwKEAjwm7jKBRDE2_H
_t8DVxzISJACwS9WbSzUlrQ8FPJvSadoN5Ig0IRDO0zfFEL5
XEmMSrGPxVhoClkbw_wcB>

Petsmart
<https://www.petsmart.com/reptile/live-reptiles/snakes-
turtles-and-more/chinese-water-dragon-15383.html>

Kingsnake
<http://www.kingsnake.com/>

Animal Specialties
<http://www.animalspecialties.com/>

List of Breeders in United Kingdom

Preloved UK
<http://www.preloved.co.uk/classifieds/pets/reptiles/all/uk/chinese+water+dragon>

NewsNow UK
<http://www.newsnow.co.uk/classifieds/pets-animals/chinese-water-dragons-for-sale-uk.html>

888 Reptiles UK
<http://www.888reptiles.co.uk/460.html>

Trovit UK
<https://products.trovit.co.uk/pets/water-dragon>

Back Water Reptiles
<http://www.backwaterreptiles.com/agamas/water-dragon-for-sale.html>

Underground Reptiles
<https://undergroundreptiles.com/shop/baby-chinese-water-dragon/>

Tricias Water Dragon
<http://www.triciaswaterdragon.com/>

Chapter Four: Requirement before Buying a Chinese Water Dragons

As you pour through these pages, gather nuggets of vital facts on reptile care and husbandry and what is and will be required of you to provide your new water dragon a nurturing, safe and conducive environment.

It has been determined by herp experts in the animal field of medicine that most ailments, malaise, diseases and poor health conditions are due to the incorrect set up of reptile enclosure.

Poor lighting exposure, improper humidity ranges, incorrect temperature settings, and unsanitary enclosure conditions are usually, if not definitively, the cause, reason and culprit of ailments in captive reptiles.

When a water dragon gets sick, a keeper should investigate the conditions inside the reptile's enclosure. A clean environment has no room for bacteria, fungi, molds or viruses to thrive. Therefore a responsible keeper should learn that this, first and above all, to be the most important rule to follow and abide in order to give the reptile the best and highest chance of surviving and thriving under their care.

Your Chinese water dragon will need quite a bit of supplies outfitted in its enclosure for it to live well, healthy, long and happy.

We'll determine and detail the what's and whys as well as the how's of proper enclosure setup which will provide your new pet water dragon a habitat that will not only provide a well-balanced shelter of comfort but also a space which promotes proper conditions to maintain good health.

Chinese Water Dragons in the Wild vs. Captivity

In their natural environment out in the wild the Chinese water dragon has been observed to be able to thrive outdoors living, existing and feeding off the land for about a decade and a few years. Out in their natural habitat of the wilderness, Chinese water dragons are conspicuously exposed to a range of different situations which a captive water dragon wouldn't have ever experienced if it were bred locally.

The Chinese water dragon will have to be on the move daily and be away from its lair in search of food by foraging and hunting for its nutritional sustenance with little to no certainty about the success of gathering enough food to sustain its daily nutritional requirements. The possibility of not being successful in gathering a sufficient amount of food to satisfy the Chinese water dragon's hunger is very real. Without enough to eat, and when there is a lack of food, which it would require, the balance of its health is comprised. Not getting its needed balance of nutrients will not immediately result in the starvation of the water dragon but deficiency on a ongoing basis can cause the water dragon to be vulnerable to a host of ailments.

Another reason why Chinese water dragons in the wild live a shorter lifespan than their captive counterparts is the presence of predators. Aside from the competition of other water dragons seeking out the same food, predators are real danger water dragons have to face.

Besides having to compete for the same diet with other water dragons which share an area of territorial hunting grounds, predators of water dragons are drawn to the area where water dragons are aplenty. The stress of dealing with and escaping predators is cause for the reptile to become hyper alert and anxious, if they are lucky not to become a larger animal's dinner. Cats, dogs, large birds and snakes prey on Chinese water dragons when opportunity for the predators is present.

Sickness and disease in the wilderness is challenge water dragons will have to experience by themselves without medical attention, a situation that their captive cousins will hopefully not have to endure.

Out in the wild an ill or diseased water dragon has no way of getting medical attention or treatment. The dragon will then have to exist the rest of its days bearing the illness in silence as it dodges the animals that prey upon it.

The length of life expectancy of the Chinese water dragon in captivity radically spikes because of available medical care when attended by the expertise of herp vet, giving the captive water dragons a higher likelihood of living healthy and well.

And because they have their keeper guardians who attend and provide for their care and nutritional needs, water dragons are spared from ever experiencing the tedious often dangerous task of hunting and foraging for food. If provided with optimal care, Chinese water dragons in captivity can live a long life of about 11 to 15 years. There are even a few who live even longer past the 15 year mark.

Housing Requirements

You should provide a minimum of at least two thermometers in the enclosure, placing one on the cool side of the space, and positioning the other thermometer on the warm side of the enclosure.

Improper ranges of temperature in the water dragons' enclosure can cause and be reason for your water dragon to become sick of a respiratory infection or make it more vulnerable to other common ailments because of weakening of the immune system and inappropriate digestion of nutrients from food due to slower metabolism.

Experiment with various light wattages, or place your water dragon's heat sources on a thermostat or dimmer switch to get the temperature just right. There is no one single rule to lighting and wattage of bulb to use inside of your water dragons enclosure as his will all depend upon the temperature of the room where the water dragon is residing. If the room is generally cool then you will need to setup a higher wattage of basking light. If the room is kept relatively warm then you could probably do with a couple of low wattage basking bulbs to heat the water dragon's enclosure. The lights must be placed on a timer so that your water dragon will get a right amount of photoperiod exposure.

The best lighting and most optimal for your water dragon's proper digestion and blood circulation is natural unfiltered sunlight. Sadly it is unfortunate because many keepers of water dragons are unable to provide natural sunlight for their pets due to a number of factors; the most obvious is they have no control of the amount of sunshine or the length of sunlight duration. Schedules also get in the way.

Chapter Four: Requirement Before Buying a Chinese Water Dragons

It's important that the keeper provide UVB in the form of fluorescent lighting. Incandescent bulbs are not acceptable as these do not produce UVB rays required by your water dragon pet.

The water dragon will need UVB to produce vitamin D3 so it can properly absorb the calcium in its diet. If it is without this lighting your water dragon will get very low amounts of calcium from the food and supplements which you are providing it and will quite likely develop Calcium Deficiency of herbivorous and omnivorous reptiles or MBD (metabolic bone disease) which is basically a calcium deficiency,

Keep in mind that you need to provide a UVB light source so that the water dragon is able bask under it. The UVB light must be set up so that the Chinese water dragon is no more than 10 inches away in distance from the light source whilst basking, or the effects of the UVB light will significantly lessen the further away the water dragon is from the light source.

The keeper will also need to outfit the enclosure with at least one or a maximum of two basking lamps for the water dragon. You may choose any incandescent light of either a specialized basking lamp or a regular bulb.

You will probably have to get different bulbs of different wattages to provide the right amount of heat and warmth; anywhere from 50 watt to 150 watt bulbs. These lights can get pretty hot so make certain that your water dragon can't get too close to these.

The enclosure should also have good ventilation and the temperature must be on a gradient. So if the top of cage is warmer or cooler, or if the enclosure has a warm spot and a cooler side the dragon can thermo-regulate. Ideally the basking area should be the warmest but the water dragon will require a cooler area in case one spot gets too hot. The keeper must provide and position a couple of thermometers in the enclosure to measure the temperature in different enclosure areas.

Save a fairly large space for the water your dragon will need by using a large plastic container. Use a container which is large enough for the water dragon to enter and exit the water basin easily, and be sure that it is filled with enough water in order for the water dragon to immerse itself to up until 50% of its body height.

Maintenance

Make sure that the enclosure is cleaned out regularly. A good once over every week will suffice for weekly maintenance but make it a point that you take the time each month to do a general cleanup of the enclosure. Remove all fittings and furnishings as well as soil and substrate. Clean out the enclosure properly by scrubbing all nooks, crannies and corners with water and organic solutions and allow it to dry well.

Replace the soiled bedding with a fresh bed of substrate and refit all fixtures and furnishings back making sure that there are no loose wires or ill-fitting fixtures which may fall on your water dragon.

Check that all the heat sources are in proper working condition and that you get the enclosure back to the proper temperature at all sides and corners. Replace the water in the basin daily with fresh filtered water but not before you have cleaned out the basin well.

Heating

Daytime temperatures within the enclosure should be between 84 and 88 Fahrenheit (28.9 C - 31.1 C). Throughout the night time, enclosure temperatures should range between 75 and 80 Fahrenheit (23.9 C - 26.7 C).

Humidity

Mind that you maintain a humidity level within the enclosure at a level of 80%. Be sure that you mist the enclosure regularly or furnish the enclosure with plants that will aid in the humidity level required within the enclosure.

Lighting

Provide and outfit the enclosure with UVB light sources in the form of fluorescent lighting. It is important that the light sources in the enclosure are at least 10 inches away from the water dragon's reach to avoid burning accidents.

Substrate

A keeper can use a combination of orchid bark and soil however the water dragon may accidentally ingest some of this substrate material whilst eating food items resting on the substrate bed. Alternatively you may use AstroTurf, but remember to melt or bind the edges and corners so that the little pieces of green fiber don't fray because this may be mixed in with the food your water dragon eats.

Ingesting of substrate runs your water dragon the risk of becoming ill with its digestive track getting impacted, this is a potentially serious issue.

Costs of Housing Requirements

If you are a first time reptile keeper it will be important to find items you will need to outfit your water dragon's enclosure with all the things it will require to live a healthy existence as well as a comfortable one.

If you have the money to spend then buying from a pet supply store would be the easiest way for you to get the job done. It will cost a pretty penny, but you could also employ the services of an experienced vivarium builder and simply give directions and specifications of what you need for the enclosure to be outfitted with.

Average costs of a brand new setup will run up anywhere from $350 - $1,500 for the enclosure, UVB bulbs and light fixtures, dimmers, timers, thermostat, thermometers, heaters, vents, water filtration system, humidifier, and basking lamps. This would also include your initial supply of substrate and furnishings like ramps, branches, any plants and additional accessories and sundries like a quarantine tank for when your water dragon is ill and needs to be separated from the enclosure it may share with another water dragon.

As early as now, start imagining how the enclosure would look. Design your vivarium and do not leave out any of the essentials that will be needed by your new pet dragon. Check out flea markets which is a great place to find some of the things that you will need at a prices that won't break the bank. You could spend as little as $100 a $350 if you choose to purchase items at a garage sale or at a flea market and set up the enclosure by yourself.

If you choose to buy second hand items make sure that you clean out each item well before you set up the vivarium. You wouldn't want to take home a perfectly healthy water dragon only to have it fall ill because you were too lazy and forewent all necessary measures of ensuring the prime safety of the enclosure fit for the habitation of your new water dragon.

Chapter Five: Nutrition and Feeding

It goes without saying, but we will anyway, that the quality of food a living being takes in is relative to the health it will enjoy and serve as the foundation of its future health and wellness. This holds true for anything that breathes and that would include your future pet Chinese Water Dragon. Understand and find out the nutritional needs of the Chinese Water Dragon to be able to raise your soon-to-be water dragon pet in this chapter.

Feeding your Chinese water dragon the proper balanced diet it needs is going to be the backbone of its future health. As with any living being, the quality of food you provide your Chinese Water Dragon will dictate the future ahead of it.

Here, the keeper will read about the water dragons' proper diet and nourishment, the correct way of feeding it, and how frequent your water dragon should be fed. In addition to what water dragons should be fed in captivity, it will interest the keeper to discover what a Chinese Water Dragon would normally hunt and eat in the wild.

Food in the Wild vs. In Captivity

Being the arboreal creatures Chinese water dragons are healthy eaters and therefore dexterous hunters and foragers. In the wild they are able to hunt for and thrive on crickets, mealworms, earthworms. In captivity they will have quite a different selection of food for their diet.

Nutritional Needs of Chinese Water Dragons

Mealworms, crickets, earthworms, wax worms, grasshopper, locusts, butter worms, other people try small feeder fish like goldfish and it may also do your Chinese water dragon a portion of finely chopped fruits and vegetables - which should make up about 10 - 15 % of the water dragon's diet. You can also research on other foods with a good ratio of calcium and phosphorus content.

Adult dragons must be offered and given all of these food examples above plus King Mealworms also called, Zophobas. Supervise and monitor these feedings because these worms are liable to bite back. Some keepers squash their heads before feeding them to their water dragons, newborn hairless mice also called pinkies and slightly older baby mice which are just starting to get hair are called fuzzies.

Insects which are contain relatively high phosphorus and low in calcium, but do contain nutritional values if not fed in large amounts or as the water dragon's main diet. A lot of insects also possess a tough indigestible exoskeleton which could cause your water dragon bowel impaction should it be fed these insects in large quantities. All insects must be gut loaded with a well-balanced serving of veggies and possibly even some calcium and vitamins before being offered to reptiles.

Insects which are fairly easy to buy like crickets, mealworms, super worms, King Mealworms (Zophobas), wax worms and earthworms. Insects which can on occasion be purchased locally or may be bought by mail order are butter worms, locusts, hissing roaches, cicadas, grasshoppers and silkworms.

Primary Foods

Earthworms are relatively high in calcium, and are fairly well balanced in nutrition. They are also soft so the danger of impaction is lessened.

Whole prey food products are typically high in calcium and protein, and because the calcium content must be included as part of the diet. Carnivorous reptiles like water dragons must be given and fed pre-killed whole prey once in a while. Rodents like mice are preferable to small fowl like chicks, but chicks are a better choice over fish. However, if mice, rabbits, rats, rodents, and chicks comprise the bulk portion of the water dragon's diet, then there should be no need for vitamin and mineral supplementation.

It must be that newborn pinkie mice have less calcium than adult mice. If this is the case, then a calcium supplement is to be added to the diet of the water dragon.

A variety of whole prey food products would range from young chicks, pinkies, fuzzies, and adult mice, rat pups, and feeder fish like minnows.

There are keepers who also offer lizards like anoles to their water dragons as a source of nutrition.

Tips on How to Feed Chinese Water Dragons

Here are some tips on how to feed your new pet:

- Do not feed your water dragons live prey which may struggle and fight back which could cause injury or wounds to the water dragon

- Offer food with a pair of tongs and not with your bare hands lest it mistake one of your digits for food.

- If feeding your adult Chinese water dragons with live prey, the prey must be eaten within 24 hours of the purchase or these will expire soon after purchase.

- Watch your water dragon during feeding time lest it ingest the substrate where the prey lies.

Amount Required for Chinese Water Dragons

The answer to the discussion with regard to the frequency of feeding your Chinese water dragon as well the amount of food you are to offer will vary greatly depending on the size of the water dragon. A good rule of thumb is to offer and feed it only the amount it will acceptably eat. Each water dragon's appetite will vary greatly from each other. Have a feeding journal and document your own observations of what and when the water dragon eats. Maintaining a journal will allow you get to know the amount of food your water dragon consumes at various stages of its growth.

The feeding frequency of your water dragon will largely depend on the reptile's age. Juvenile Chinese water dragons must be fed and eat more frequently than adult water dragons to promote a healthy growth significant to and relative to its health. On the other hand, adult water dragons will notably require fewer feedings.

Juvenile water dragons would typically require daily feedings, while the mature water dragon would possibly only require to be fed every two to three days. You may also feed your adult water dragons daily if you prefer, just make certain to keep the portion sizes small to avoid the dragon from putting on the pounds and becoming overweight. And never forget to always give your water dragon plenty of fresh, clean drinking water in addition to a well-balanced diet.

A well-balanced diet should be sufficient and would be enough to provide your water dragon with adequate nutrition. However you may still opt to periodically offer supplements. The most usual supplement demanded for the wellbeing of your Chinese water dragons is calcium. Calcium is extremely vital because if your water dragon does not receive the right amount of calcium in its diet, the deficiency will lead to develop a metabolic bone disease that could be debilitating to the water dragon. Avoid this from being a reality by dusting a little amount of calcium powder over the water dragon's food at least two to three times a week at the most.

Finally, always make certain that your Chinese water dragon's food source is sanitary and healthy. Purchase feeder insects and tiny rodents like fuzzies, and pinkies from a pet store or pet supply merchant, or raise them yourself. This is the best method of safety to employ in order to keep and prevent your water dragon from contracting internal parasite infections.

Make certain to thoroughly wash all vegetables and fruits well with clean water before offering and feeding them to your water dragon, or you could opt to buy organic, to avoid the ingestion of pesticides and other chemicals which are harmful to the reptile.

Chapter Six: Handling Your Chinese Water Dragon

Handling your Chinese Water Dragon is the start of how a potential keeper begins training their water dragon. Exposure to a variety of different sorts of situations is an important learning that your water dragon will have to undergo in order for it to thrive better. In a large way, this is also how a water dragon, and you, begins to get to know and get used to each other.

Keep in mind that no two water dragons are alike and that each individual will display their own traits and behavior according to theirs, but your training will make an impact on how it will interact with you and other people as it grows. It will need to be let out of its enclosure once in a scheduled while to allow it to stretch out and get a good brisk workout because you wouldn't want to limit your dragon to a tiny enclosure its entire life - and quite a long one at that.

Reptile keepers of water dragons have each their own techniques which work for them, whilst others had to learn through hits and misses. Your patience will be required because you want to gain positive results from the experience and rushing the process of handling and training isn't going to result in success. We'll discuss how you can make the process of handling easier for you and your water dragon in this chapter to prepare and allow you to set expectations so you have a solid idea of what to do and anticipate during this period of getting to know each other.

The probability of being scratched, nicked, tail-swished at, reared up on, or nipped at by your water dragon is a reality that could happen and this has been true for many reptile enthusiasts. Remember that the Chinese water dragon also has its own defense mechanism it averts to when it has to face changes and this is a good time to remind you that the water dragon is perhaps one of the most friendly of water dragon sorts and whatever posture-threats it may display is simply that, a threat.

Water dragons do not understand the concept of glass; hence, you might want to rethink that glass vivarium. They seem to think that glass is something they can eventually break through because many keepers have witnessed their water dragons ram, slam and bang their snouts onto the glass. This can be a stressful everyday situation if not addressed early on, even before your new actively playful buddy gets to your doorstep.

As you start out on this path of caring for a water dragon or two, go over this section contents well because not only will we discuss why it will be vital to socialize your dragon, we will also share best practices and steps on how to handle your dragon whilst minding your and your reptile's safety.

Remember that the more it sees you, the more it hears your voice, the better socialization results will be. When you first bring the new guy home and whilst allowing it time to settle in, call out to it, talk to it gently from the other side of its enclosure and allow it time as well to see you do the things you normally do.

You want to make sure that you only take your water dragon into rooms which are warm enough for it and importantly, reptile pet-proofed. Make sure that the water dragon is comfortable above all, before allowing it to roam in select areas of your house. Make sure it has no access of escape as chasing after your dragon could easily be a scenario you may face.

Every reptile keeper was once a novice and had to learn how to handle their reptile pets with proper care. There are a number of ways your water dragon could get hurt, injured or in distress if the keeper has no clue about the water dragons' physical limitations. Get ahead of your own reptile-training skills and know what can be dangerous to your water dragon if improperly held and posed.

Tips on How to Handle Your Pet Properly

How about we keep this bit of the section streamlined and simplified? Sound good? Now, do remember that you and your pet will develop your own special dynamics as days, weeks and months pass.

Your investment will go beyond the initial costs of purchasing, transporting (if the water dragon of your choice will be coming from out of state or country), housing setup, enclosure furnishings and fixtures, an extra enclosure for when the water dragon is ill and needs to separate from the healthy population (if your collection of water dragons multiply) vet and medicine bills and daily provision of food.

A responsible keeper of a new Chinese water dragon will need to factor in the time they will need to allot for the care, observation of the reptile pet. The keeper will also need to set aside a considerable amount of time and spend time and effort in making sure that the habitat of the water dragon is kept under sanitary conditions which is optimally required to maintain the wellness and health of the water dragon.

Sacrifices will also be needed from the water dragon keeper and these sacrifices would have to include foregoing some of the things you are used to having around the house once your socialized and house broken water dragon is allowed to roam areas of your home freely.

Further research on the subject of handling is advised but more so, hands on experience will teach you and reveal much more about each other. Let's start with rooms you want to share with your water dragon.

Proper ventilation will provide a good airflow around the enclosure which will help in reducing fungal growth, and making sure that the enclosure will not overheat especially during summer or hot days. A good airflow will also benefit the growth of live plants inside the terrarium.

Reptile Pet-Proof Rooms

- Make sure that your pet can roam around freely inside its enclosure, and has a secure door. An open door, to your water dragon, is an invitation to explore further and a good way for a keeper to lose sight of the dragon.

- Block out any gaps beneath the door with a towel.

- Block hidden spaces, such as the gap between a low table or bed and the likes, which have a tight gap in between floor and furniture because it will be difficult for you to reach in and collect your water dragon if it decides to stay under that area.

- Use a plastic socket cover to conceal any unused sockets.

- Survey an area before allowing your water dragon to roam. Are there spaces too low between furniture and floor? Would it be easy for you to rescue the water dragon if it slips under that? Will you have to move heavy furniture to get to it? If this so, rethink this area of the house and stick to where it can roam without getting caught under furniture.

- Ceiling to floor curtains will look inviting to the water dragon and it may try to climb it. You can replace them with shorter curtains or fold up the curtain away from the floor and fasten it high.

- If it still makes attempts to reach up and climb the curtains you can either rethink this room or change your window coverings with blinds.

- Rooms with too much furnishings is probably best avoided whilst the water dragon is young and smaller.

- When it is more mature you can reintroduce your water dragon to these rooms by allowing it short, supervised visits throughout its period of growth.

- Make sure to remove any toxic plants in the room that would pose harm to the water dragon lest it ingests it.

- Make sure that there are no objects that your pet could topple, fall over and hurt anyone or the water dragon. Remove any of these objects which could be potentially dangerous to the household and the water dragon.

- Water dragons are arboreal and will try to get high up to survey its surroundings. Consider bringing in a hibiscus tree or two and place them in the rooms where the water dragon will be allowed to roam freely. This will be a better attraction, if not safer, than climbing your curtains.

- If the water dragon is allowed more than a couple of hours to roam free outside its enclosure, make sure that the temperature in that room is more than adequate for the water dragon.

- You may consider making a small investment on a portable heater to warm the room whilst the dragon is in there.

- You can also get a heating pad or two where the water dragon can go to and heat itself.

- Study the places your water dragon seems to prefer over others and consider placing basking lights using UVB fluorescent tumb lamps in those areas.

Correct Handling Methods

- If you are bringing home a young dragon, best allow it on its own, inside its new digs to have it get used to the new living conditions.

- Your water dragon will likely display signs of stress when you first bring it home and this is just natural. This will change as it begins to settle into its new home and starts feeling safe.

- Your water dragon has no concept of glass and will ramp on the "invisible" wall in effort to explore the outside.

- Provide extra protection to your water dragon from itself and cover the lower most parts of the vivarium with a cardboard, cloth or thick paper, high enough that the world outside is out of your water dragons vantage when it rests on the floor of its digs. This will lessen the stress factor and make for an easier to deal with social-trainee.

- When you are confident that your water dragon has shown to be at ease initiate physical interaction and get its attention by first giving it a friendly wave from outside its digs.

- Having caught its attention, slowly introduce your hand inside the enclosure and give it a stroke or two to make sure that it isn't nervous.

- If it is skittish, or if it keeps trying to make a break from you or shows signs of more than usual distress it is best to abandon the idea and start again later.

- If it shows no signs of resistance to your hand being in its digs, reach out to where your water dragon and then, with one hand, gently scoop it up from its underside or belly, lift it up and out with your other hand supporting its back without squeezing it.

- To ensure further safety, with your thumb, forefinger and middle finger, cuff the two front legs of your water dragon and as you gently speak, and lift the dragon out of its vivarium.

- Make sure you are not holding its legs too tightly or it will struggle to break free.

- Always be gentle with your grip.

- While it gets used to being in your hand, you may start examining it gently because this is a good time to take mental notes of its physical attributes and condition you too will be a new idea to your water dragon, so keep this in mind because your water dragon may choose to get to know you as well by climbing on you - allow it to do so and continue to speak to it gently as it does can set it down on a table inside the room of its enclosure.

When it begins to display much more ease and comfortability about being outside its home with no resistance to you or your touch, you may begin taking it around your home to give it a tour in rooms where you have a reptile pet-proofed.

Allow it the luxury of getting used to the larger surroundings and give it time on its own to explore at no instance should you attempt to lift your water dragon by its tail as this may result in avoidable injury under no circumstance, and this is strongly stressed - none at all.

Turning over the dragon on its back constricts the lungs of the water dragon making it difficult for the dragon to breathe. The dragon on its back may look like it is sleeping but it isn't, it maybe slowly running out of breath being on its back.

Chapter Seven: Breeding Your Chinese Water Dragons

A large number of these reptiles still come from and are imported from their native lands to satisfy its demand in the pet trade. However, there has been a notable increase of captive breeding by seasoned hobbyists in Europe and North America which has helped in staving off the problem of illegally import and export of the water dragon.

Dragons caught in the wild display behaviors of distress due to the trauma of being chased after and caught. It has to go through the confusion of one minute being in the wild and minding its business to dealing with nets, constricted often times crowded cages, uncomfortable transport methods, and rough handling. All these pose as a reason for the water dragon to be hyper-alert and defensive.

Captive breeding is a good solution to stop the promotion of wildlife hunting and poaching. It allows for a newly hatched water dragon a better advantage to socialize with ease.

It is also important to remember that female water dragons, especially the sort who are expected to be gravid at one point or another of its adult life, need special care attention and most of all would need a vivarium of its own outfitted for the purposes of laying her eggs in peace and away from the general population of your reptile collection. .

A female water dragon must be provided with a proper area where the female can lay her eggs. Should a female water dragon develop eggs and isn't provided with the necessary conditions she would need and what she would consider a proper and rightful place in order to lay her eggs, the female may hold them from getting laid and she would become egg bound. This could lead to the death of the female water dragon if this problem is not identified and discovered quickly.

The developments of eggs take a great deal of toll on the female water dragon's body. The female will need to be in perfect condition to get through this period with a clean bill of health. The gravid female water dragon will need to be fed a highly nutritious diet. She would also need to be housed in a vivarium at the optimal and proper temperatures during this time. In addition to all the special need of the female during this egg-laden period while she is gravid she must also be provided with a sufficient intake of calcium supplements every day.

In order to develop strong bones during this period when bone and the developing egg shells are vulnerable, the female Chinese water dragon will need calcium supplements which will be a vital requirement to shell the eggs. If she's not getting enough calcium from her diet and not exposed to the proper UVB fluorescent lighting which is another important necessity to help absorb the calcium properly, the female water dragon will begin to use the stored calcium from her bones and could become calcium deficient.

This chapter will deal with the sexing of Chinese water dragons, their mating habits, how you can help to initiate mating, the breeding process, caring for a female carrying eggs, how to help build a suitable nesting place for the egg-carrying female water dragon, the labor period for the female water dragon, incubation period until hatching, how many clutches (or eggs) are to be expected and the frequency or seasonal breeding periods.

You will want to take careful note of this chapter, and strive for further research, if you are planning to expand your collection or help toward the prevention of water dragon poaching from the wild.

Breeding Basics

Water dragons are usually ready to mate when they are about 2 years old. Identifying males from females while they are still young can be tricky. Some have been lucky enough to stumble upon the discovery with a new set of hatchings from what a keeper may have once thought to be a male water dragon.

Describing the differences in males and females by mere sight is easier on paper than it is in actual life. Many seasoned keepers once did not have ideas of how to tell the dragons apart until the Chinese Water Dragons reach full maturity; this is when visible differences begin to show apparent. Males will be longer and heavier than females. Males will have larger heads compared to that of a female water dragon. Chinese water dragons are generally considered mature dragons once their chins display their mature colours (refer back to the chapter where we discussed the growth stages and appearances of the water dragon).

If you feel the necessary need to know at an early stage and can't wait the little over two years it will take for these visible adult markings to show then get in touch with your herp vet and discuss this. The procedure requires the water dragon to be poked and prodded with a long, relatively thick, needle-like probe which is inserted in their reproductive areas. This will not be a pleasant experience for any of the water dragons.

This is where your contact with a seasoned herp vet comes in because you will not want to carry out this identification procedure on your own even after you have had enough experience seeing an expert to do it right. Gender identification of reptiles is called sexing. Sexing a reptile is not as easy as looking down its "private areas" for clues and visible signs. It is a delicate process which if not done right will hurt the water dragon. At any rate, no self-respecting herp vet will agree to sexing water dragons under 18 to 20 months of age or shorter than two feet long.

Let's now discuss mating and let you in on some important details you need to know and watch out for when water dragon gender has been established.

Water dragons can be prepared for breeding by hibernation. Make sure that the dragons have reached the proper age of two years old and have a length of about 3 feet for males and 2 feet for females. Make sure that they have been taken to the vet annually for physical checkups and that they are in good health.

During the period between late fall or early winter, the keeper has to reduce the dragons photoperiod exposure from 12 to 14 hours of daylight to 10 hours of daylight and 14 hours of darkness. The temperature in its enclosure throughout the (induced) day must be lowered to 75 - 78 Fahrenheit, remembering to keep a warmer area beneath an incandescent lamp which is able to give off temperatures reaching 80 - 84 Fahrenheit. Night time temperatures should be reduced to 68 - 74 Fahrenheit. The duration of reduced light and lowered temperatures should last for about two months.

If your water dragon has been feeding on a daily basis, which is the recommendation of most successful water dragon keepers, you will need to reduce their feeding during this hibernation period to once every week.

When the two months of the hibernation period is up, place the Chinese water dragons back on their regular photoperiod of 12 hours of light, with day temperatures ranging between 84 -88F and 75 - 80 F throughout the night. Increase their feedings back to their normal once a day.

When male water dragons are put back on their normal schedule after hibernation they almost immediately show breeding readiness behavior. It will start to chase after the female dragon, bob its head, attempt to mate with the female by grasping the female dragon by its nuchal crests with its teeth and twist her so he can penetrate her by inserting the hemi-penis. This process will usually last between 10 to 20 minutes.

On occasion female water dragons will get stressed by the experience, hurt and/or injured during the breeding period if the male is too persistent. If the female displays behavior's akin to stress or does get injured it is best to move the female dragon to another enclosure for a little while until she has been able to recover and calm down.

Nesting Requirements

Female Chinese water dragons could produce and lay eggs whether or not she has mated with a male dragon. If the female has not been with a male the eggs will naturally not be viable. Female dragons carrying eggs in her belly is called a gravid dragon, this is the dragon equivalent of pregnancy,

The gravid female dragon's appetite will decrease as the eggs fill her and her belly expands, so eating will be a problem for her. Not getting the sustenance she needs because of the eggs may have her appear emaciated. During this period, it is important for the female dragon to have daily doses of calcium in order for the eggs to gain strength. When the gravid female starts exhibiting plumpness around its belly area put in a lay box, a deep enough container which can hold 10 - 15 eggs, filled with peat moss or moist soil, inside its enclosure to get it ready for the next stage. The ready female will dig then proceed to burrow a hole in the box, much like they do in the wild, to bury the eggs she lays.

Next let's discuss incubation of the eggs. Once the eggs have been laid, carefully lift, remove and transfer the eggs to an incubator. Place the eggs in vermiculite at a distance from each other. Cover a portion of 2/3rd of the eggs and maintain the incubator temperature at 84 -86 F. Be sure that you missed the eggs every couple of days to maintain incubator humidity.

A female dragon who has laid fertile eggs will officially become a mother after 60 - 65 days of successful incubation. Hatchlings should arrive then. When this happens, move the hatchlings to their own enclosure and feed them the insect diet discussed earlier in this book.

The males and female newly born siblings should be separated by around 3 to 4 months. You can differentiate a male from a female by its tail lengths although it may not be accurate. Ask your vet if you want to know how to identify their sex.

Chapter Eight: Life Stages of Chinese Water Dragons

In this chapter, you will learn about the life cycle or life stages of Chinese Water Dragons. These creatures, like most reptiles have interesting way of coming about, so why not take the time to learn how they were born, how they grow, and all the things in between! If you wanted to breed Chinese Water Dragons in the future and raise these baby creatures, this chapter can be essential for you as a future reputable breeder!

The Life Cycle of Chinese Water Dragons

When hatchlings emerge they come out into the world at an impressive length of 5 to 6 inches from snout to tail. These young water lizards prefer to group amongst themselves and away from the adult population.

The Chinese water dragon will shed its skin several times throughout its lifetime and this is quickly replaced by an impressive brand new body suit, sporting colors appropriate for the water dragon's specific age.

Sometime between the juvenile age periods to the water dragon's adult stage of life, the water dragon will develop and show a colored patch, of stark contrast to its bright green body, on its neck which signals the near adulthood or full maturity of the water dragon.

In addition to the notable and visible changes the water dragon goes through as it continues to mature, the dragon's head will also be notably larger during its growth process. .

Once they have reached the age of maturity both male and female water dragons will have a fully developed nuchal crest prominently on their backs. The male water dragon's nuchal crest will visibly be higher and longer compared to that of the female water dragon.

The male water dragon will also have a fully developed mid sagittal crest which will prominently be displayed on the top of its large, triangular head and this mid sagittal crest will help it thermo-regulate and allow it to find suitable basking areas amongst the other things this special male water dragon feature can do.

Chapter Nine: Diseases and Health Requirements

When in the wild, it serves a sick reptile no good purpose of displaying weakness. In nature, the pecking order dramatically shifts when a sick animal is sensed by other animals - an animal, considered a predator, can quickly be free game to stronger animals. A show of weakness is communicated as an invitation to predators, saying "eat me".

Being the future keeper of the strikingly beautiful and exotic Chinese water dragon, the responsibility of spotting subtle shifts in its appetite, behavior, habits, and appearance along with other more telling signs of malaise will fall on your shoulders. The following sections of this book hope to detail signs and symptoms of the onset of illnesses the water dragon could develop, contract, or get and common medical conditions to which the reptile may be prone. More importantly, our aim to minimize the probability of your precious Chinese water dragon falling ill is what this book wishes to stress above all.

This is a good time remind the responsible reptile keeper of the importance of providing a sound diet consisting of a good balance of all vitamins, nutrients, minerals your pet water dragon requires.

Common Illnesses of Chinese Water Dragons

Internal Parasites

Captive bred water dragons are likely to be contaminated with internal parasites through cross contamination from other infected reptiles or via ingestion of some food items. An infected water dragon can show stress and begin suffering from other ailments which may overwhelm the water dragon causing it lethargy, decreased or lack of appetite, loose smelly frequent stool or diarrhea, and a failure to thrive. This requires an immediate visit to your herp vet who may recommend a stool examination to determine the sort of parasite the water dragon may be suffering from in order to prescribe the proper medicine.

Metabolic Bone Disease (Hypercalcaemia or Hypocalcaemia)

The causes of this very serious disease is lack of calcium or very high levels of phosphorus in the water dragon's diet, it could also be that it has not had sufficient UVB exposure or inadequate exposure to formulated fluorescent tube light. This could also be caused by improperly setting up its enclosures required lighting and heating needs.

Reptiles require to be housed at their correct temperature setting in order for them to digest their food successfully, and hence absorb their required calcium and other vital nutrients in the food items properly to thrive best. Symptoms of this disease include spontaneous bone fractures, skeletal deformities, muscle tremors, and inadequately calcified eggs.

Rostral/Snout Damage

This is shown by water dragons which have been housed in enclosures which are either too small, or in glass walled enclosures. Since water dragons have no concept of glass they see the outside world as a place to explore and will, even after failure, continue to pursue the outside by banging against the glass panels of its vivarium. Injuries could result to torn skin, damaged tissue and bone infection which could lead to death.

Prevent your water dragon from banging its snout up against the glass panel by covering the bottom half of the vivarium with paper, cloth or cardboard in order for the outside to be concealed when it is at floor level of its vivarium.

Mouthrot or Stomatitis

This condition is frequently displayed by Chinese water dragons with snout damage, or systemic infections caused by improper environment settings or stress. You will want to prevent further damage to the snout by visiting your herp vet at the soonest possible opportunity because ignoring this can result to a series of infections which could lead to death.

Gastroenteritis

The symptoms of this ailment would include listlessness, diarrhea, loss of weight, and loss of appetite.

Your water dragon could die if this ailment is ignored and left untreated. If your dragon is showing any of the symptoms mentioned above take it to the herp vet immediately and have its stool tested for protozoan, bacterial or worm infections.

Respiratory Infection

This ailment is commonly caused by inadequate enclosure heating, and when a water dragon is kept in an environment under stressful conditions. Symptoms include listlessness, swollen appearance of the body, reduced appetite, and as the infection progresses and worsens it would frequently gape its mouth followed by occasional forced exhalations.

Take your water dragon to the herp vet immediately if you see any of these symptoms displayed by your water dragon, which will perhaps have the water dragon take antibiotics. On your end, you should increase the water dragon's enclosure temperature to 85 - 88 Fahrenheit around the clock until the symptoms are completely gone.

Mite and Tick Infestation

Mite and tick infestation is a typical medical issue with water dragons, as with other herps for that matter, which have been housed in inadequately poor conditions during shipping, or in crowded over populated pet shop enclosures. There is a very high possibility of likelihood that your water dragon may in fact have some ticks and or mites on it on the day you take it home.

If the ticks and mites are given the opportunity to thrive they will become quite challenging to get rid of, and will in fact stress your water dragon to the point of it falling ill, not to mention that a very awful infestation of mites and ticks on your water dragon could cause a severe blood loss, and extensive skin damage.

Fungal or Bacterial Infections

On occasion a purchased water dragon may have skin which is infected by a bacterial or fungal growth. Bacterial and fungal infections are typically caused by being housed in spaces which are too damp or it could be that the water dragon's previous living conditions were poor or not properly sanitized and this warm and moist condition which they love is the prime condition where fungi and bacteria will grow and spread.

Should you notice or suspect that your pet water dragon has a fungal or bacterial infection you must bring it to a qualified reptile vet to get a proper checkup and diagnosis.

The vet will most likely recommend giving the infected water dragon an antibiotic or anti-fungal cream to apply on the areas affected with the skin disease. You will need to clean out the dragon's enclosure thoroughly and meticulously disinfect branches, furnishings and fittings along with the dragon's water container and soak basin with a mild bleach solution.

Remove the old substrate and replace the substrate and any other cage furniture that is easily replaceable so as to limit the spread of further infection. Coupled with a topical antibacterial or anti-fungal ointment the water dragon could be bathed in 80-85F chest deep water which has betadine, an amount enough to make the water a medium tea color, for a half an hour per day for a period of two weeks.

The spots will visibly improve gradually over time, but it may take a shed or two before the once infected area appear healthy once more.

Tips on Taking Care Your Chinese Water Dragon

The Chinese water dragon is not the easiest reptile to care for in terms of its temperature, lighting, humidity needs, but it most certainly is one of the most strikingly beautiful reptile sort and is worth each and every extra effort.

For one, the Chinese water dragon requires considerably large habitat, with both terrestrial and aquatic features. It will require a sizable tank for a single dragon which can hold 75 gallons (285 liters), this is the minimum size.

However, a much larger is better and highly advisable; the growth rate of the water dragon may be slow but it will be quite a considerable size once it reaches maturity and it will need all the space it can have in order to thrive well and healthy. Should you plan on keeping multiple dragons, the enclosure must be at least 4 feet (1.22 m) in length and 5-6 feet (1.5 – 1.8 m) tall.

It is much smarter to start housing your water dragon in a larger enclosure than to change and upgrade later as your water dragon grows, so don't scrimp on this investment or cut corners because doing so will have you ending up spending a lot more money in the long run.

In order for the conditions inside the water dragons enclosure fit its needs and to promote healthy growth and wellness, maintaining the right temperature and humidity levels in your water dragon's enclosure is paramount. In order to come close to replicating the Chinese water dragon's natural environment, you must need to maintain a daytime temperature of 80 degrees Fahrenheit in its enclosure, and a level between 70-80 percent in terms of humidity, and a nighttime temperature should be no colder than 75 degrees Fahrenheit.

Maintaining a clean and sanitary enclosure is another important foundation to the wellness and overall balance of good health to your water dragon.

A poorly setup and haphazardly "cleaned" enclosure is an invitation for a host of viruses, bacteria, and fungi to thrive in and spread. Keep in mind that an ounce of prevention is worth a pound of cure and stick by this adage.

Your discipline in keeping and maintaining a clean enclosure equates to savings on medical bills and reptile medicine cost. A potential keeper also wants to remember that a water reptile infected with a disease could potentially pass on the malady to other reptiles in your collection which would cost much, much more than if the measure of cleaning and the investment of time toward maintenance were employed instead.

Chapter Ten: Quick Summary

You've learnt what you can, and you are encouraged to do more research about the Chinese water dragon and heed the advice within these pages. Be reminded that the Chinese Water Dragon isn't all that easy to take care of but with your commitment and patience, you and your new buddy will get your own groove on, and get the hang of each other in no time. You want to go ahead and get a good seasoned herp vet in your court before you actually close a deal on the acquisition of your water dragon.

We began this book with the promise of providing you detailed information of everything related to and beneficial to raising your Chinese Water Dragon.

Reading this book maybe fun but it can also be time consuming. So in this chapter, we have compiled all the essential topics, and points provided here to summarize the information you need. You can check this for a quick glance if you forgot some important detail, so that it can be easier and convenient for you.

Are you now ready to have your own Chinese Water Dragon pet? I'm sure you are!

Points to Remember

Before we close this book you have to remember the two most important things that your Chinese Water Dragon really needs. Remember that the habitat you build for your soon to arrive bright green buddy will need to meet the right temperature, humidity, lighting, substrate, and water requirements. Another is the importance of giving it a healthy balanced diet throughout its life.

Secondary, but all equally important is the socialization and handling requirements of the Chinese water dragon; your patience, time, sacrifice, and commitment will play a real large part of the success of you raising your own Chinese Water Dragon. We trust that you and your new buddy will have many years to enjoy together!

Now, here's a quick overview of everything you've read. Consider this as a quick reference guide in relation to the Chinese Water Dragons origins, the steps to acquiring one, the requirements for its habitat, nutrition, socialization, husbandry, and everything iin between.

Biological Information

- **Scientific Name:** Physignathus cocincinus
- **Country of Origin:** Southeastern China, Thailand, Vietnam, Cambodia, Laos
- **General Appearance:** Bright green colour with, green and brown banded tail, mature length is approximately 3 feet for males and 2 feet for females
- **Maturity:** reaches maturity in 2 years or when it has reached maximum adult length
- **Longevity:** 10-11 years in the wild; 12 - 15 years in captivity

Chinese Water Dragons as Pets

- **Behavioral characteristics:** shy and guarded at first but warms up easily. Can bring on an attitude when in unfamiliar situations but is able to adapt quickly and well with proper handling and socialization
- **Pros/Cons:** A charming pet with friendly amiable traits and has own individual personality from each other but needs quite a bit of requirements that need to be met in order to thrive well.

Purchasing and Selecting a Healthy Breed

- **Where to Buy:** may be bought from backyard breeders or previous water dragon owners
- **Characteristics of a Healthy Breed:** generally, the water dragon should have no eye discharge, must be alert, active, mobile and easily adaptable
- **Characteristics of a Reputable Breeder:** Choose a breeder who has had success in breeding the animal and who is ready answer questions for you and be as equally eager to know about your intentions for the animal

Requirements before Buying a Chinese Water Dragon

- **Living in the Wild:** Can be found along river banks, rainforests; prefers to be where there is permanent water supply and where trees are abundant
- **Housing Requirements:**
- **Cage Size:** 4 feet (1.22 m) in length, and 5-6 feet (1.5 – 1.8 m) tall, or preferably bigger, if possible
- **Where to Place:** place low on the floor away from direct sunlight if using a glass vivarium. If otherwise, placing vivarium near sunlight source is ok.
- **Accessories Needed:** UVB lighting, heaters, vents, humidifier. Aquatic plants, substrate, branches, laying box, quarantine vivarium
- **What to Avoid:** handling too soon after acquisition and introduction to new home, handling by the tail
- **Cleaning Frequency:** weekly maintenance; monthly general cleaning

Maintenance/Husbandry

- **Heating Temperature:** Daytime temperatures should be in the range of 84-88 degree Fahrenheit (29-31 degrees Celsius), with a basking spot of up to 90 degrees F (32 degrees C). At night, the temperature can safely drop to 75-80 degrees F (24-27 degrees C).

- **Humidity Temperature:** 80 %
- **Lighting Temperature:** UVB light, 12 hours on, 12 hours off for a day/night cycle
- **Substrate Temperature:** none

Nutrition and Feeding

- **Food in the Wild:** woodworms, earthworms, crickets, earthworms
- **Food in Captivity:** crickets, mealworms, waxworms, earthworms, grasshoppers, butterworms, locusts, and possibly small feeder fish
- **Nutritional Needs:** protein, calcium, D3, vitamins and minerals
- **Feeding Tip:** do not introduce food with your bare hands, do not feed it live food (mice) in case of struggle
- **Feeding Ratio:** young dragons are to be fed small meals everyday, juveniles can be given bigger portions and fed one every other day, adults can be fed everyday, portion dependent on size and weight

Handling Your Chinese Water Dragon

- **Tips on how to handle your pet properly:** avoid handling the Chinese water dragon soon after bringing it home; allow it to get used to its new surroundings first

Breeding and Requirements

- **Incubation Period:** 64-68 days
- **Clutch/Average Number of Eggs:** average of 3 clutches or around 6 to 7 eggs
- **Frequency/Season:** once a year upon maturity, late autumn
- **Nesting Requirements:** lay box filled with soft moist soil deep enough that can be dun into
- **Size of Enclosure:** 10 gallon vivarium
- **Accessories Needed:** UVB lighting, basking lights, thermostat, thermometer, heaters, vents,
- **Enclosure Temperature:** 80 Fahrenheit

Diseases and Health Requirements

- **Health Tips:**

  o Get the services of herp vet before acquisition

  o In order for the conditions inside the water dragons enclosure fit its needs and to promote healthy growth and wellness, maintaining the right temperature and humidity levels in your water dragon's enclosure is paramount.

  o Maintaining a clean and sanitary enclosure is another important foundation to the wellness and overall balance of good health to your water dragon.

  o A potential keeper also wants to remember that a water reptile infected with a disease could potentially pass on the malady to other reptiles in your collection which would cost much, much more than if the measure of cleaning and the investment of time toward maintenance were employed instead.

- **Common Illness:** Internal Parasites, Metabolic Bone Disease (MBD), Hypercalcaemia or Hypocalcaemia, Rostral/Snout Damage, Mouthrot or Stomatitis, Gastroenteritis, Respiratory Infection, Mite and Tick infestation, Fungal or Bacterial Infections

Glossary of Important Terms

Anterior: head or the front end of a species

Autotomy: A defensive mechanism wherein reptiles voluntarily shed their tails when they feel threatened to save themselves from predators.

Caudal: It is the tail end or refers to the reptile's tail.

Cloaca: A tube-like structure for fecal or urinary waste and other reproductive discharges like eggs or fluids

Cold blooded: An animal that cannot regulate its own body temperature and metabolic function and only relies on external environmental conditions.

Crest: A decorative ridge of spikes or skin usually found on the necks, backs, and/or tails of reptile species.

Dewlap: A flap or fold of skin found on the throat of some reptiles. It generally stretches from the chin to the chest. It is also used during territorial or aggressive displays.

Dorsal: It is referred to the top part or back of an species mostly opposite of ventral.

Dysecdysis: A condition when a shed is abnormal or incomplete.

Ecdysis: The natural process of shedding skin to allow for growth.

Ectothermic: other term for cold – blooded animals.

Endothermic: Other term for warm – blooded animals. Such species can regulate its own body temperature and metabolic function.

Fracture plane: Regularly spaced sections between or in the middle of vertebrae in a reptile's tail where breakage occurs during autotomy.

Jacobson's organ: It is mostly found in the roof of the mouth that allows reptiles that "smell" with their tongue to detect odor or other things like predators etc.

Keel : A ridge down the center of a scale.

Lateral: the sideview or side part position

Parotoid glands: These are paired glands that looks like huge bumps on a reptile. In some animals, it is where they secrete toxic substances used for self-defense.

Parietal eye: An organ found on some reptiles usually at the top of their heads. This organ can detect light and is active in prompting hormone production. It also assists with thermoregulation. Sometimes it is referred to as pineal eye or third eye.

Posterior: the rear or hind end.

Setae: It's a tiny, hair-like projections mostly found on toe pads of some reptile animals. This allows reptiles like lizards, iguanas, water dragons and the likes to walk and climb on vertical surfaces, such as glass, and even ceilings.

Snout-tail length (STL): Standard measurement of a reptile from the tip of its nose to the tip of its tail.

Snout-vent length (SVL): Standard measurement of a reptile from the tip of its nose to its vent, or anus.

Thermoregulation: It is the process of self-regulation of a species' body temperature by moving between warm and cool parts in their habitat.

Vent: The outside opening of the cloaca that connects it to the anus.

Ventral: It is the bottom or stomach part of an animal.

Index

A

antibiotics.. 109. 110. 111. 112

appearance...3, 11, 15, 41, 111

attention..77, 78, 87

B

black 6, 8, 21, 116

body........................... 6, 13, 14, 21, 22, 50, 70,76,77, 79, 80, 85, 90, 92, 110, 112

breeder......................... 30, 37, 40, 41, 42, 43, 44, 45, 47, 48, 51, 53, 62, 86, 89, 92, 102

breeding 1, 10, 13, 15, 33, 41, 43, 85

brown 6, 29, 69, 116

brushy...24, 117

C

capable 7, 17, 22

captivity.. 6, 24, 32, 35, 63, 101, 103, 110,

captured 6, 17

care..1, 3, 5, 25, 28, 30, 36, 40

choosing 7, 40, 45, 62

colors...5, 6, 28, 41, 81

companion 7, 30, 121

contrasting 6

covers 8

D

E

F

G

M

N

O

P

R

S

T

Photo Credits

Page 1 Photo by user PublicDomainPictures via
Pixabay.com,
https://pixabay.com/en/lizard-dragon-reptile-animal-22258/

Page 5 Photo by user InspiredImages via Pixabay.com,
https://pixabay.com/en/chinese-water-dragon-2326614/

Page 15 Photo by user InspiredImages via Pixabay.com,
https://pixabay.com/en/chinese-water-dragon-male-chinese-2044695/

Page 29 Photo by user NicholasDeloitteMedia via
Pixabay.com,
https://pixabay.com/en/lizard-dragon-zoo-2133996/

Page 43 Photo by user InspiredImages via Pixabay.com,
https://pixabay.com/en/water-dragon-chinese-physignathus-1512969/

Page 56 Photo by user InspiredImages via Pixabay.com,
https://pixabay.com/en/chinese-water-dragon-reptiles-lizard-1952179/

Page 65 Photo by user InspiredImages via Pixabay.com, https://pixabay.com/en/chinese-water-dragon-lizard-dragon-1545486/

Page 77 Photo by user InspiredImages via Pixabay.com, https://pixabay.com/en/water-dragon-chinese-physignathus-1513040/

Page 86 Photo by user MK1_FIESTA via Pixabay.com, https://pixabay.com/en/chinese-water-dragon-asian-green-1726507/

Page 90 Photo by user InspiredImages via Pixabay.com, https://pixabay.com/en/chinese-water-dragon-lizard-dragon-1545409/

Page 100 Photo by user InspiredImages via Pixabay.com, https://pixabay.com/en/chinese-water-dragon-lizard-dragon-1545390/

References

"Are Your Chinese Water Dragon Ready for Breeding" – ChineseWaterDragon.net

http://www.chinesewaterdragon.net/select-ready-breeding-chinese-water-dragons/

"Australian Water Dragon" – Wikipedia.org

https://en.wikipedia.org/wiki/Australian_water_dragon

"Breeding Chinese Water Dragon" - Tricia's Water Dragon
http://www.triciaswaterdragon.com/breeding.htm

"Care of the Chinese Water Dragon" – Tricia's Water Dragon
http://www.triciaswaterdragon.com/dragoncr.htm

"Chinese Water Dragon" – Waza.org
http://www.waza.org/en/zoo/choose-a-species/reptiles/lizards-and-tuatara/physignathus-cocincinus

"Chinese Water Dragon" – Wikipedia.org

https://en.wikipedia.org/wiki/Chinese_water_dragon

"Chinese Water Dragon" – The Spruce

https://www.thespruce.com/chinese-water-dragons-1239191

"Chinese Water Dragon Care Sheet" – NewMedia Retailer

http://assets.newmediaretailer.com/243000/243794/chinese_water_dragon.pdf

"Chinese Water Dragon Care" – Reptiles Magazines

http://www.reptilesmagazine.com/Chinese-Water-Dragon-Care/

"Chinese Water Dragon - Physignathus Cocincinus" – Petmd.com
http://www.petmd.com/reptile/species/chinese-water-dragon

"Chinese Water Dragon – FAQ" - Tricia's Water Dragon
http://www.triciaswaterdragon.com/faq.htm

"Common Health Conditions Affecting Chinese Water Dragons" – ChineseWaterDragon.net
http://www.chinesewaterdragon.net/health-concerns-common-medical-conditions/

"Is My Water Dragon Sick?" – Chinese Water Dragons
http://chinesewaterdragons.tripod.com/id6.html

"Looking for a Complete Resource on Breeding Chinese Water Dragons?" – Chinese Water Dragon
http://www.chinesewaterdragon.net/complete-resource-on-breeding-chinese-water-dragons/

"Reptiles Now More Popular Pets than Dogs" – Telegraph UK
http://www.telegraph.co.uk/news/earth/3500882/Reptiles-now-more-popular-pets-than-dogs.html

"The CITES Appendices" – Cites.org
https://www.cites.org/eng/app/index.php

Feeding Baby
Cynthia Cherry
978-1941070000

Axolotl
Lolly Brown
978-0989658430

Dysautonomia, POTS
Syndrome
Frederick Earlstein
978-0989658485

Degenerative Disc
Disease Explained
Frederick Earlstein
978-0989658485

Sinusitis, Hay Fever,
Allergic Rhinitis Explained
Frederick Earlstein
978-1941070024

Wicca
Riley Star
978-1941070130

Zombie Apocalypse
Rex Cutty
978-1941070154

Capybara
Lolly Brown
978-1941070062

Eels As Pets
Lolly Brown
978-1941070167

Scabies and Lice Explained
Frederick Earlstein
978-1941070017

Saltwater Fish As Pets
Lolly Brown
978-0989658461

Torticollis Explained
Frederick Earlstein
978-1941070055

Kennel Cough
Lolly Brown
978-0989658409

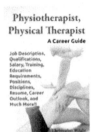

Physiotherapist, Physical
Therapist
Christopher Wright
978-0989658492

Rats, Mice, and Dormice
As Pets
Lolly Brown
978-1941070079

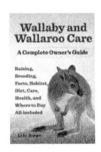

Wallaby and Wallaroo Care
Lolly Brown
978-1941070031

Bodybuilding Supplements
Explained
Jon Shelton
978-1941070239

Demonology
Riley Star
978-19401070314

Pigeon Racing
Lolly Brown
978-1941070307

Dwarf Hamster
Lolly Brown
978-1941070390

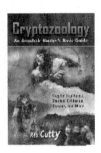

Cryptozoology
Rex Cutty
978-1941070406

Eye Strain
Frederick Earlstein
978-1941070369

Inez The Miniature Elephant
Asher Ray
978-1941070353

Vampire Apocalypse
Rex Cutty
978-1941070321

CPSIA information can be obtained
at www.ICGtesting.com
Printed in the USA
LVOW13s0052150917
548754LV00014B/357/P

9 781946 286420